REFLECTIONS

OF EVE

AND HER DAUGHTERS

by Marsha Newman

WELLSPRING
Concord, California

ACKNOWLEDGEMENTS

Special acknowledgement must go to my husband, Gene, first, for the idea of a book written about the great women of the Bible from their perspective; second, for his support in freeing my time so I could write; and last, for sharing with me the joy of the poetry. He is my best admirer and my best critic. His appreciation of my work spurs me onward to reach for the best within myself.

TABLE OF CONTENTS

I. REFLECTIONS OF EVE

Memories of Heaven 1
Thoughts in the Garden. 6
Beyond Eden. 9
Eve and Her Children 11
Lamentation 13
Psalm of Thanksgiving. 16
Ode to Life 18

II. REFLECTIONS OF SARAH

Love Song 23
On the Journey 25
The Desert, My Teacher 26
In Egypt 28
Here is Hagar. 29
The Psalm of Sarah 30
Isaac - Laughter of Joy 32
To Hagar. 33
Parting. 36
Farewell to Abraham. .37

III. REFLECTIONS OF RUTH AND NAOMI

Call Me Mara 41
Of Love and Loyalty. 42
Devotion 43
Homecoming. 44
The Stranger 45
In the Fields 47
My Daughter 48
A Single Woman, Alone. 49
A Kindly Man's Delight. 50
Dear Boaz 51

IV. REFLECTIONS OF MARY

A Royal Line. 55
On the Road to Bethlehem 59
In the Stable 61
Birth of a Child. 64
Discovery 66
Sacrifice 67
The Quenching 68
The Master Builder 69
Joseph, a Father 70

Transported 71
Leavetaking 73
Elder Brother 76
On His Miracles 77
Anguish 79
Reflections of Mary 81

Illustrations, by Jazelle Lieske
A Father's Blessing 4
Sarah and Isaac 34
Ruth 46
Mary of Nazareth 58
Reflections 72
Anguish 78

This book is dedicated to Eve, Sarah, Ruth, Naomi and Mary, in appreciation for their exemplary lives. It is also dedicated to all women who have sought role models of righteousness in attempting to understand life and to live their lives for God.

REFLECTIONS

OF

EVE

MEMORIES OF HEAVEN

They say that when we reach earth the memory of our first home will fade, and we will not remember this life. Oh, I wish it were not so! It will be hard to be separated from my loved ones. In defense against such a time I will record a few of my most precious memories.

I am a child of the universe.
Through all my consciousness
I had seemed to float
Like stardust
Through the galaxy,
Til Father came, and drew
My spirit aspects from all
The infinite deep.
I came from mist and shadows,
Gathering light
And fire
And form,
And passed from filament
To spirit,
And felt my Father's arms
Enfold me in His love.

Never again in
All of life's eternity
Will there be such a moment!
He filled my being
With such power
And joy surpassing
That a flash of fire
Flamed out across the sky,
And I became a child of God
Who once was nebulae.

The centuries rolled forth
Engulfing me with love and beauty
All my childhood days
While Mother nurtured me,
Teaching me the ways
Of Godhood in embryo.
She gave me from her womanness
A deep wellspring of gentleness,
And a knowledge of my holiness
As her beloved child.

Some years we walked the clouds,
And kicked up firmament
For our play.
She showed me how to twine
My hair with star chips.
When I broke my heart
Over my own childish faults,
She kissed me with her tender lips.
Mother! Oh, Mother mine,
How can I leave you
Even for a few years,
Even for a minute?
How could my world be beautiful
Without you in it?

And then the time
Of counseling —
Father and Jehovah
With the noblest of my brethren
Made plans for earth's creation;
And though our brother,
Lucifer, rebelled,
And fell from grace,
Taking many spirits
With him into space,
The promise of our next estate
Brought Heaven-wide jubilation.

With all His children gathered about
Father drew Adam out,
Ordaining him a prince,
The father of Man to be.

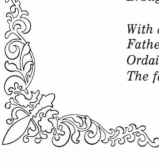

Then Adam searched the throng,
Looking long
For a bride.
With penetrating gaze
He searched, and found my eyes,
Then holding out his hand to me
He called me to his side.

"Bring forth Eve!"
A tremor seemed to shiver
Through my very being.
The children of God
Passed on the word
Like a priceless treasure,
In whispers gathering depth
Until the infinite sky
Rang with their jubilant cry.
"Bring forth Eve,
Mother of souls,
Creator of new life."

Then came the singing.
It pealed forth from
Innumerable voices.
My brothers and my sisters,
Whom I have loved forever,
Came forward one by one
To give us their sweet blessings,
For we shall draw their spirits
Down to earth,
And help them fill the destiny
Of their souls' eternal worth.

Once more Father's arms
Enfolded me,
Fusing godly power in my soul.
Then he placed His hands
Upon my head.
"I give to thee a blessing,
Even a Father's blessing," He said.

Jazelle 81

"Eve, my precious daughter,
Thine is a supreme calling
As a Woman.
Upon thee rests the hopes,
The needs of all mankind,
So fill thou well
The measure of thy creation.
Let thy delight be in thy husband,
And thou shalt one day be
The queen mother
Of a great nation.
Let all thy devotions be to me,
And in thy life's decisions
Choose thou, carefully.
Increase thy knowledge,
Acquire understanding,
And practice with great patience
The lessons of earth life."

Then His voice broke,
And once He faltered
Before again he spoke.
"Knowest thou I love thee, Eve,
With a perfect love,
And will that thou
Come back to me one day.
Do not forget, sweet daughter,
Thy Father's heart is tender
And He anxiously will
Help thee on thy way.
Come back!
Come back in triumph,
And I will crown thee queen,
And such a jubilation
All Heaven hath not seen."

THOUGHTS IN THE GARDEN

In the warmth of the day
We go walking . . .
I try not to crush
The flowers,
Abundant at my feet.
Adam sometimes tucks them
In my hair
So I can smell
The soft fragrance there.
I did not know
There would be such beauty
On earth,
Although I should have guessed,
For Mother said
That Eden is the bower
Where she and Father
Oftimes rest.

There is a small lake
Snuggled between
Two mighty trees.
It's grassy banks allure me,
And I can see the blue sky
In the still lake's
Quiet face.
Once I looked there,
And saw my mother
Peeking from behind a cloud.
I clutched my heart
In unfamiliar pain,
And cried aloud.

My body sometimes
Feels strange on me.
I do not understand its ways.
Yet I have learned to love
The feel of velvet petals
On my lips
And raindrops on my cheek;

The vision of a slivered moon
As through the clouds it slips,
And shadows chasing moonbeams
Hide and seek.
O how beauteous is the world
Our Father gave us!
Such a gift is almost more
Than I can comprehend.
How wise of Him
To also give me Adam
To share my thoughts and pleasures,
My dear husband,
My only friend.

Adam! Adam!
See how luscious golden fruit
Is beckoning us to eat . . .
But why not that tree?
It is the loveliest,
And one of the creatures
Said its fruit was sweet.
Oh yes! That's right.
I do remember that Father
Said it was forbidden,
But I wish
He had not placed it
So near by.
For some odd reason
I do not understand
It draws my eye.

We have yet only seen a few
Of the creatures God created.
I know by name the timid deer,
The family of rabbits,
And, of course, the birds;
They wake me every morning
With their song.
Yesterday I felt a fish
Slither through my hands
As he glided along.

Many creatures, small and furry,
Tiny busy bodies, scurry
Between the trees,
And lace the grass
With faint paths on their way.
Strung along the flower leaves
Are spider webbings,
Luminescent on a dewy day.

Of late
I have had strange longings.
Loneliness lurks nearby,
And when I think of heaven
Sometimes I cry.
Dear Father,
Do not think me ungrateful
If at times I long for thee,
And mother, and home.
Some days I wander all alone,
And seek Thee
At the meadow's fringe of trees,
Or behind a hilly dome.

More and more
I seem to sense
That there is something dear
missing from my life
As Adam's wife.
We are incomplete.
I know not how,
But more and more often
I find within my soul
A mysterious impatience now.

BEYOND EDEN

The sky is heavy,
Ladened with wild clouds
Across the valley floor.
Rain is moving
In heavy sheets
Relentlessly toward
My flimsy door, ·
And Adam is yet abroad.
It frightens me
To have him so long away.
The thundering gruff voice
Of the storm
Hurls me backward
In my mind to that awful day
We came here
To this lonely world.

Forever shut out from Eden!
Beautiful primal home
Of my soul!
Never more to revel
In the perfume of thy blossoms
Or sleep secure
On a grassy knoll.
Eden lost!
In one wretched, fearful dream
Of wild confusion,
Of storm and plummeting
Through space,
Rejected and expelled
From Father's grace,
Because of me. . .
     Thrust through time
And galaxy
Far from His throne.
Because of me
Exiled from our home!
Bitter, biting winds
You cannot scathe me
More than the lashes
My own thoughts gave me.

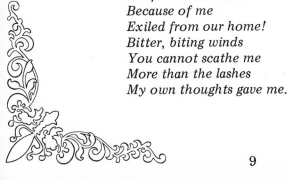

For I was a disobedient daughter,
I who had thought
I would unerringly be true
To my beloved Father.
I promised Him
That I would do
Whatsoever thing He asked of me,
Then forgot, straightway,
And tasted of the forbidden tree.

Knowledge!
It was called the tree
Of knowledge!
O what dear price knowledge,
And for such bitter fruit!
My poor Adam
Must have loved me dearly
To follow suit.

I almost died then
Of shame.
Father said that we
Should surely die.
So foolishly to disobey
His counsel I wished
That I, indeed, might swiftly die
Instead of facing Him.
And though, still we breathe,
These lonely years
Without Him ever near
Have been a death most grim.

Will we ever find our way
Back to Heaven now.
Two little children who
Wandered in their play,
We struggle, hand in hand,
And wonder how
To find the path
That leads us home.
Oh Adam, come soon!
I cannot bear to be alone
In such a solitary home.

EVE AND HER CHILDREN

- I -

This downy head
Suckling at my breast
Is all the perfect love expressed
Of God and Man and Heaven fled.

Father sends them,
Reminders of my eternal home.
Though through a blighted world I roam,
My children bend my thoughts to Him.

Complete now!
The strange stirrings of my soul fulfilled.
My body's lonely whispers stilled,
Though care has creased my brow.

Childish laughter
Mocks earth's wide expanse outside my door,
And I love this child more than all before,
Yet not as much as those to come hereafter.

- II -

For I am a fountain
   Of eternal creation,
   Where Life bubbles up
   In a never-ending surge
   From the inmost, garden part,
   The warm mysterious womb of me,
   A Woman.

I am as eternal
   As the star-strung heavens.
   The surge of life within me
   Begins, struggling in joy,
   Mounting in exhilarating expectancy,
   And bursts forth,
   A mighty offering of love
   And innocent beauty to the world,
   My Child!

I am the rising song
  Of Alpha, of Eternity,
  Of Past, Present and Future.
I am the teacher of songs,
The artist of new life,
The creator of love and vision,
For a fountain leaps eternal
Within my private,
Unknowable being,
A Mother of Souls.

- III -

Would that I
Recalled more clearly whence we came
Before the serpent whispered first my name,
But all is veiled since Eden was put by.

Still I teach
My children all I know of God's plan,
Obedience, devotion, nobility of man,
And eternal joy within an earnest reach.

This tiny fist
Pefectly modeled after mine!
Oh, I did not merit such sweet love divine,
Or guess that babes should be angel-kissed.

Come thou my soul's delight,
And mend my heart with thy more holy light!

LAMENTATION OF EVE

Shall eternity thrust
Its grisly hand,
And tear my spirit
From my soul!
My sons,
My precious jewels,
Swallowed up
In the evil hole
Of murder.
No, no,
I shall not let it be,
Else terror
And black, black grief
Smother me,
S m o t h e r   me . . . .

Cain, Where is thy brother,
Thy gentle brother Abel?
Cain, Cain, What of the years
You sat with him at table,
And picked together berries,
And roamed together valleys,
And mingled childish laughter
Over childish sallies.

When did I fail
To teach you love?
When did you fail
Righteousness to learn?
After such a deed
Where did you think to go?
Where is there now
For you to turn?
For God will cast you out
As He did once His daughter, Eve.

Now is it my turn to know
How a parent's soul can grieve
Over children lost
And children dead!
Oh, Cain! Abel!
I see you yet,
Sweet babies
In my head!

And the wind takes up
my keening.
Hear his shrill voice
Screaming in the plain.
That wicked, wicked Satan
Steals my darling sons,
For falsely spoke he to you,
And, jealously led my Cain
to utter destruction.
All my happiness
In my children now hath run
Out upon the thirsty sand
Consumed by a burning sun.

Tears
come
and
come,
and
someone
lifts
me
from
beside
my cold,
dead son.
Dear Abel,
Sweet, angel boy,
Ever, ever still my joy.

Tears
flow
and
flow,
and I
turn
to go
with Adam,
And
there is Cain,
Another son slain
by sin.
Needing me
he cries out;
And I,
A mother,
With arms about,
Shield him for a moment
From his pain —
My poor,
Lost,
Cain.

EVE'S PSALM OF THANKSGIVING

Lift up O heart
Thy praise unto the Father!
The measure of our creation
Is forever joined
With the glory of the earth.

Praise unto thee
O Father of our souls!
It is for our children,
And their children after them
That thy hand did shape the world
And all that gives delight therein.
All the tender flowers
That perfume the hill's cheeks
Were made for my dear babes.
All the sweet breezes
That tremble the trees,
All blown with thy breath
For the joy of these,
The sons and daughters
Of thy handmaid Eve.

The earth and all its marvels,
Reflections of a Celestial mind,
Created and given
As a special place of learning.
KNOWLEDGE — a burning
Knowledge of good and evil.
LOVE — Love of good not evil.
For knowledge leads love
Gently by the hand,
And my heart lifts up
In oblation to so great a plan
Where God can draw nobility
From the soul of man!

The Master of the Temple
Of divine Truth and Light
Breaks the lock
Thrusts open the door,
And floods our darkest night
With the brilliance of His Love.

16

Oh how my soul rejoices
In the mercy of our God!
What wisdom
In the Father
To give us choices!
What graciousness
To give us freedom
(Though darkened paths
We oftimes trod.)
And earth is our choice!
Even after all!
Even though we fall,
And weep,
And lament our birth.
Heaven is our home,
But earth the training field
Which sometime, tried and tested,
Will a harvest of young Gods yield!

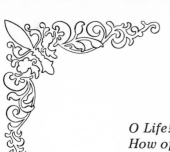

ODE TO LIFE

O Life!
How often have you filled me
With wretchedness and pain,
Until my tears were oceans,
Tossed with tempest, wind and rain.
Then quicker than a hummingbird
A rainbow 'round me sewn,
And the Dove of Hope came winging,
And to my weary hand hath flown.

O Life!
Too often loneliness has shamed me
Into faithless tears and doubt,
And I have pleaded with my Father
To put the beggars all to rout.
Then surely comes His word of love,
And suddenly I stand
Strong in courage, great in hope
When He but takes my hand.

Dear Life!
How sweetly have I loved thee
Despite capricious ways
That alternated dark and light
To challenge all my days.
And sweetly must I leave thee now,
Thy savor on my breath,
And I shall taste its loveliness
Even until death.

Farewell, farewell,
My old friend and teacher, earth.
I go back to the Father of my soul
To wait the resurrection's birth
When thou and I shall be made whole.
Then all the wickedness that plagues thee
Shall be swept from thy dear face.

Enwrapped in God's own glory
Shall thou roll through boundless space,
And I shall be thy queen again,
And walk thy vales and hills
As once I did in Eden
Till my heart's joy overspills.

Farewell dear friend, but not for long.
Eternity is our rendezvous, and Heaven is our song.

REFLECTIONS

OF

SARAH

LOVE SONG

After many years came Abram, treading the idols of Chaldea like an angry lion, roaring in the ears of the unrighteous, the forgotten word of the Lord Jehovah. Chaldea reeled with the power of his words and the strength of his righteous soul. The priests of Nimrod plotted among themselves to rid the land of so fearsome a man. Only a woman, I had no power to offer him in service of his cause. Only a woman! How I wished I might have gone with him to battle the great beast of evil that sat upon the people demanding sacrificial blood.

Oh, Abram - his name resounded through my mind like a clarion call. Would that I might multiply myself a thousand fold into an army of mighty men of God, and sweep away the evil all about me that I have endured so long. All the days of my life have I walked veiled to hide my countenance from the glances of Nimrod's men. Some have pitied me, and guessed some gross deformity I hide behind my cloaks and veils.

Few Chaldeans remember now the words of our Father Noah. Few remember to honor him, and fear his God. But Haran, my father, taught us the words of Jehovah, and to remember our tribal fathers even unto Shem who was the son of Noah, even unto Adam who was the son of God.

Much of my life have I avoided society. All I have known of joy is the whispered lullaby of the wind through the high grasses of grain. All I have known of love is the heavy golden moon that holds the face of my beloved before my wondering heart. Now comes Abram, and I know at last the good wisdom of patience, of faithfulness unto the Lord.

Abram - I have heard my father speak his name so that I seem to always have known him. Abram - Beloved of my Father; beloved of the great patriarch, Noah; beloved of God; and beloved of His handmaid, Sarai.

Abram - thy star is my hope, thy name is my dream, thy life is my joy, and my love repents that I was not born of thee as Eve from father Adam.

Abram,
Though many years
My womanhood lay sleeping,
Desire comes softly
Through the darkness creeping,
And ever through the lonely years
God's spirit brushes away my tears,
And whispers one name in my ears --
Abram!

In my ear a voice
Hath whispered all my days
Abram ---
Abram.

The song birds weave
A melody of heavenly praise
of Abram ---
Abram.

My Father speaks of Abram,
Man of God,
Child of promise,
Youth of strength,
Constant as a prophet's rod.

I save my dreams of love.
I store my hopes and joy.
I hold my tenderness
A sacred treasure
For one man to enjoy ---
Abram!

ON THE JOURNEY

Now the Lord spake unto my husband, Abram, and we did leave forever the valley of Chaldea. Notwithstanding it being a land of much wickedness, nevertheless, it was the land of my birth, the country of my childhood, a green and fertile land that was most pleasing to the eye.

With Nahor and Milcah, with Lot and grandfather, Terah, we departed out of Chaldea, traveling ever northward, following the great river Euphrates. There also went forth all of our servants and their families. And the Lord blessed us with much prosperity. Our flocks increased; our cattle and our goats became great herds.

Surely the Lord, Jehovah, hath smiled upon us and opened the blessings of this earth unto us. Only one thing doth He withhold from us—posterity for Abram. My soul is cast down in deep sorrow while my prayers are raised high continually for this much cherished blessing. A child, yea a son! My heart would delight in a daughter, fair and tender as moonlight on the river. Yet Abram needs a son to carry on his lineage, a son to share his priesthood, a son to claim the birthright of his father.

We travel in rich and fertile valleys, and all the creatures of God are increasing and filling the measure of their creations. Our she-goats give suck to their kids. The calves follow closely their mothers. My maid servants suckle their little ones, laughing and clasping their babies to their hearts, while I alone look on in barrenness.

O Father, dear Father of my soul, must thy daughter Sarai cast down her eyes in shame before her lord Abram. Must he be denied the gift of posterity because he took Sarai to wife! And how can such a sweet love as ours not bear delicious fruit. In the lonely hours of the night when his dear head rests upon my heart, my tears flow down upon my pillow. Abram, my beloved, you should not have chosen your Sarai. Another wife would have given you greater blessings - though never so great a love!

Where is my womanhood without my babes? Where is my motherhood, the very cause for which this woman's form was made? My belly churns and sickens for want of filling. My breasts wither for lack of milk and a child to nurse. My very soul must perish in grief if my lot is to be a fruitless vine. O Lord God who made me first a woman, make me also a Mother!

THE DESERT, MY TEACHER

O come,
Thou warrior,
Golden Sun,
Strike fire across the sky.
Ascend the mountains;
Flash thy sword;
Impale the blackguard night!

The desert waits
Her fearsome love.
Darkness flees before thy stride.
Flaming sands spring up
To greet thy radiant face,
And joyful sounds
The many voices of thy bride.

And Lo!
Here waits Sarai,
Pupil of thy constancy.
The Lord Jehovah
Bids me wait,
And learn my lessons
At thy knee.

The desert -
My friend, my teacher,
Vast monument to serenity.
Everlasting sands endure
The fierce protecting cover
Of a jealous lover,
And her barrenness endures
Patiently, eternally.

I have lifted up
My pride, and served it
To a seering sun
In sacrifice to God.
What rocky altars
Hath my barrenness
Built in desert solitude
On fruitless sod!

O Lord, Jehovah,
My heart is a fertile valley,
Rich with love;
And children come
An endless stream of abundance
From above -
To all thy handmaids
Except Sarai.
What is it I
Have done to bring
So great a curse
Upon my soul?
I yearn, I plead,
I cry to give a child,
A son,
To my beloved one,
My Abram.

Like my friend, the desert,
If I live a thousand years
In barrenness,
Perhaps my soul will learn humility,
And serenity
Replace my tears
With righteousness.

IN EGYPT

Egypt is my terror! So, so much like Chaldea. I have covered my face, and draped myself with many folds of robes. We have heard that Pharoah surrounds himself with lovely girls, and takes whomever he desires; and if he must kill a husband, what of it? No one can say him nay. . .But God may!

I lean upon His promise and His word. He said to Abraham that we might go, and yet be safe. If any should ask I must fall back upon our kinship, and say I am his sister. In the ancient way I am, for I became my grandfather's daughter when Haran, my father, died. And Abraham was, for a space, my brother.

Pharoah's court is grand, and I am honored here for now, but what shall be Pharoah's rage when he discovers he cannot have me for a wife? Will my life be worth this silver earring he gave me, and will we escape with our possessions? I do not know. I only try to answer questions as little as I can. Today I was bade to stand and receive my husband while I stood at Pharoah's side. Tonight, unless God intervenes, I am to be his bride. These last days my heart has been in constant prayer. I would die here before submitting to Pharoah's love.

Is it beauty that he prizes? Then let my grace transfer to another's face and let my form be plain with no loveliness to spare. Then Pharoah would not care to steal me from my beloved. When men have not the beauty of God's spirit in their lives they search for its imitation wherever they can. But it is not given to woman, despite her loveliness to fill the void in a Godless heart.

Dear God, if you are sleeping somewhere beyond these Egyptian stars, awake and send thine angels to me quickly, or Sarai will shortly come to Thee.

HERE IS HAGAR

The years have fled, weeping.

With them goes my hope. If my husband is to have posterity it must come from the womb of another, one younger and more favored of the Lord. Abraham assures me ever faithfully that the Great Jehovah loves me even yet, and all my sorrow is to teach me patience. Does it not also teach me despair? But no, I'll not give in to despair, for one sign of weakness and the great beast will devour me! There can be no doubting our ever gracious Lord, for there is none other to follow, none other we can petition with our prayers, none other we can cling to in our sorrow. Who knows why we are called to wander this desert plain of woe? Only God, and He only tells us courage, patience, and hope.

The years have passed, one endless prayer to God, and now the beauty of youth hath passed also away. My womb is withered with the years. My only hope of children is through my handmaids, and they will count for me a gift of posterity unto my husband. Dear Abraham! Many wives could he have taken all these years, wives who would have made him rich in sons and daughters. Yet does he wait, ever faithful, for a child from his Sarai.

Abraham, how can I see another bear your children, another woman carry your seed to fruit? My heart is sick nigh unto death, and if I loved you less I could not bear the shame.

Abraham, here is Hagar.
Make of her a mother to thy son.
Only do not breathe the sweet words
In her ears
That once you swore to me,
Your own beloved one,
Sarai.

Abraham, here is Hagar,
In this at least I shall not fail.
Go quickly to her tent
And with her lie,
But when the morning glimmers pale
And draws aside eve's shadowy veil
Remember thou
Sarai.

THE PSALM OF SARAH

No other Gods have I,
My Lord, but Thee.
No other arms enfold
My fainting heart but Thine.
Who could wrest the anger
From my soul so lovingly,
And leave a pearl of joy,
And let me call it mine?

No other Gods of stone
Or silver hue
Can lead my weary soul
To hope and peace.
No other God could slake
My fearsome thirst with dew
Of distant blessings
And whisperings of strength
That never cease.

Where should I wander, Lord,
If ever I should turn away?
Are there sweeter meadows
Afar off Thou hast not trod?
And could I find the sunshine brighter
On a wayward day
That passed not by
The splendid throne of God?

No other God would bid me
Call Him "Father."
No hope have I of love
More sweet, more dear,
And I, thy child, even
In punishment would rather
Turn back, and kiss Thy brow,
And beg Thee to be near.

For all the days that stretch
So endless long,
And all the tears that dampen
My pillow through the night,
But serve to forge
Determination strong
That faithfulness will make me Thine,
And patience yet will see me shine,
A princess, dressed in
Thine own Celestial Light.

ISAAC — LAUGHTER OF JOY

- I -

Hath the world always wakened thus,
With laughter and with song!
And was I deaf and blind,
And dead to happiness so long?
Wake up! Wake up the sleepy world.
The night hath brought a child,
And left a gift upon my breast
Of rapture undefiled.

My soul,
What a fountain burst of joy
Erupts from deep within thy wells,
And laughter spills out recklessly
At what an angel tells.
Leap up! Where is the singing,
The music thunders in my ears!
Oh wide, wide world, rejoice, rejoice!
Sarah's child, her promised child,
A beautiful son appears!

- II -

Sleep, I shall not sleep.
Let him sleep, my darling boy.
Many lonely years I've had for sleeping,
But I covet now each priceless hour of joy.

Sleep, I shall not sleep
With Isaac nestled warmly by my side.
God hath made his Sarah who is old
To savor new the season of a bride.

Sleep is the thief of time
And who knoweth how long Isaac shall be mine.
He is my son, and Abraham's
But first and last, O Lord,
The years have made it clear
He is not ours, but Thine.

TO HAGAR

I did not know how fiercely anger could pounce upon my heart. I thought that these many years had wrung me dry of such juices, and left me calm in the face of puny trials once my life's great trial was ended. Oh, I did not know what a terrible face anger rears when your dearest possession, your child, is threatened. A mother is worse than any creature of the wild desert when her babe is in danger or mocked or despised.

Hagar, once I treated you harshly. I admit it was pure jealousy for your fruitfulness and misery at my own barrenness. I have ever been grateful that the angel protected you, and persuaded you to return. I would not in soberness desire to see you burn beneath the desert sun. Your son, Ishmael, has been a great delight to me as well as his father Abraham. How I would sorrow had we lost the lad and thee.

Still, Hagar, must you remember in your own fierce motherly love, Isaac now is the birthright son. An angel promised it, and God ordained it, yet Abraham's life's joy will be undone if his two boys grow up each to hate the other one. If we cannot live together in peace then will our sons grow up in strife, and, through too close a rivalry, may destroy the happiness of their father's life. If we part, let us part without hatred. It would grieve my soul. I will give to you your freedom — never more a servant, nor your son, nor his seed.

Your life shall henceforth be free, and someday, hopefully, shall your heart be freed from evil thoughts of me and hatred's bitter weed.

Jazelle 81

Janelle 1981

PARTING

Dear son,
I would speak to thee of love,
A mother's love who waited years
To wrap her soul around your own,
And wash thy cherished face
With grateful tears.
Dear son,
Knowest thou thy mother loves thee
With a perfect love, and wills
That thou should learn to know thy God,
For He is Lord
Of all earth and sky and hills,
And before that thou wast mine
Thou wast His.
And if I bring thy spirit
Back to Him
My life's grand mission has been done.

Dear Isaac,
When I am gone
Yet may you hear my voice
In the song of the dawn birds;
And the raindrops
Drumming upon the tent
Will murmur your mother's words
Of constant love.
When I am faded
And gone away into the sun,
You'll hear my laughter
Chasing before the wind
As you run.
When I am gone
Yet shall you never be alone,
For a mother's love transcends
Eternity's grasp,
And ever to her soul
Her loved ones clasp.

FAREWELL TO ABRAHAM

We are old, Abraham, my love.
What endless sands
We have walked together,
Pledged to one another 'til death
And beyond!
Were you so fond of your Sarah
That you would chance
Losing your blessing from God?
Many years you bore with me,
Waiting, waiting for my fertility,
And I was dry as sand.
You could have had me and
Many wives besides.
You were rich and strong,
And might have had anything you chose.
Yet you chose only me,
And took my burden as your own,
And went childless so long,
'Til our lives were at their close.

Well, husband, God proves us
As He likes.
My trial was in the waiting,
And yours the sacrifice.
Oh yes, I knew,
But only when the trial was past.
I think He knew
I would have cast
Myself upon the altar
In Issac's place.
I could not meet such a test
With grace.
Not after so many years
Of waiting.

Come, old man,
Lie you down beside me on the cot.
Is there anything that we have not
Been to one another?
Anything we have not shared
With each other?

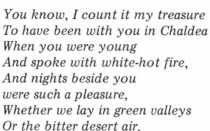

You know, I count it my treasure
To have been with you in Chaldea
When you were young
And spoke with white-hot fire,
And nights beside you
were such a pleasure,
Whether we lay in green valleys
Or the bitter desert air.

I would never tire
Of hearing you speak of God.
You've always known Him
So personally.
Now must I go before you
To meet Him alone.
Do not wait too long, my love,
To come to me.
As you waited for your Sarai,
So she shall wait for thee.

REFLECTIONS

OF

RUTH AND NAOMI

CALL ME MARA

Naomi:

I am Naomi, which is to say "sweet" or "pleasant." My parents named me so, for their days were pleasant and also their hopes and dreams for me. But God hath appointed a different course for me.

I was but a maiden when my husband took me for his own, and my life was like a white and tidy boat, drifting gently under the sleepy Bethlehem sun. And the Lord blessed us with sons. Praise be the Lord of Hosts! He gaveth me sons in Israel! I saw them grow straight and tall, obedient and faithful. I heard them laugh, and heard their shouts of strength when they wrestled about as young cubs will.

Elimelech and I were full of joy because of them, even when the famine came to Israel and food was a few grains of barley. Then he spake to me one day, "Come, Naomi. We must take our sons and go away, into the land of the Moabites, for God hath whispered this thing to me, and surely good will come of it if we faithfully obey."

So we came, out of the land of our fathers, of our God, and went unto the heathen Moabites to make our home. We found this people to be fair, to deal justly and kindly with us. And God hath blessed our home with two lovely maidens, my daughters, Ruth and Orpha. They found a place in the hearts of our sons for they were gentle and full of grace and love.

A daughter is a sweet thing, but a son is better than gold and precious gems, and behold the Lord my God hath taken them away from me, these stars in my crown. So am I left in my old age, adrift in a merciless sea, a small and shattered barge, tossing aimlessly, and the eye of the burning sun shall consume my soul. Therefore, call me no more Naomi, for those days of pleasantness are gone. The hand of the Lord hath chastened me, for what I know not. I am brought low in my sorrow in the land of strangers who know not my God and who laugh at my ways. Now must I return to my homeland, there to die, and with me my husband's name and lineage. Yea, call me no more Naomi. I take another name — the name of Mara, for all sweetness and pleasure hath turned to bitterness. Nevertheless, praise be the name of the Lord, Jehovah.

OF LOVE AND LOYALTY

Ruth:

I am Ruth. I am a Moabite woman, and have brought sorrow upon my husband's people. I have cast about in my mind to know wherefore this family of righteous Israelites has been so cursed by their God, and I can only suppose it must be because of me. They came, one day, on feet dusty with the miles from Bethlehem-Judah, wearing their strange clothing, and keeping their strange customs. It was my mother who first gave them to eat and drink, and it was I commanded to draw the water from the well. We did not understand their ways, but hunger speaks with a loud voice, and plenty cannot help but answer.

And thus it is with sorrow. We heard the woman Naomi keening with grief, for old Father Elimelech left her to death's ancient sorrow. I went to them with consolations, poor and unworthy, but it won me a place in their lives. Is it not strange how quickly pleasant sunlit paths can turn to rocky treacherous trails? For I was to wed a Moabite boy. He was my childhood betrothed, but Mahlon was my woman's devotion. He looked at me with eyes that caught my soul, a gentle bird, within the net of love's sweet emotion. Ahh, Mahlon, what evil have we done to curse your family so? Surely love is of God, yet it must be that my love was not seemly before His great eye, for surely your honor was above reproach.

Now art thou gone to touch palms with thy father Elimelech, and thy brother Chilion has fled from a Moabite love also. Naomi has become mother to me as she was to thee. Though I may have brought her this sorrow, I must follow her as a chick its mother and borrow courage from your Hebrew God, and trust His love as you have bidden me to do. Naomi is all I have left of you, my beloved, so have I bid farewell to all my childhood friends. I have kissed my own father and mother on both cheeks and bid them happiness until death. I hear not the reproaches that test my determination. For my way is now Naomi's way, our sorrows bind us as one, and naught can stay me from giving my life to her as I gave my heart to her God and her son.

DEVOTION

Naomi:

"Go, return each to her mother's house: the Lord deal kindly with you, as ye have dealt with the dead, and with me. The Lord grant you that ye may find rest, each of you in the house of her husband. Turn again, my daughters: Why will ye go with me? Are there yet any more sons in my womb, that they may be your husbands?"

"Turn again, my daughters, go your way; for I am too old to have an husband. If I should say, I have hope, if I should have an husband also tonight, and should also bear sons; would ye tarry for them till they were grown? Would ye stay for them from having husbands? Nay, my daughters; for it grieveth me much for your sakes that the hand of the Lord is gone out against me." *

Ruth:

"Intreat me not to leave thee, or to return from following after thee: for whither thou goest, I will go; and where thou lodgest, I will lodge; thy people shall be my people, and thy God, my God: Where thou diest, will I die, and there will I be buried: The Lord do so to me, and more also, if ought but death part thee and me." *

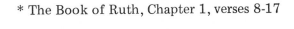

* The Book of Ruth, Chapter 1, verses 8-17

HOMECOMING

Naomi:

In Bethlehem no hand goes wanting, no stranger's cup unfilled. In Bethlehem is holy oil to soothe a fevered brow or sweeten a bitter heart. In Bethlehem are these who remember Naomi when she was rich and full with sons and husband, when pleasant were her days, and pleasant were her words, and delicious were her gifts from God.

In Bethlehem find we compassion for the hard hand of Life that smites us. Prayers will soar to supplicate at Heaven's door for Naomi, and once again will I see friends wherever my eye falls. In Moab was I kindly met, though always as a stranger. But who visits a stranger? Who laugh and makes light of daily trails with a stranger? Who remembers long-time hurts and last season's joys with the stranger in town?

O how I am weary of polite and empty talk as always greets a stranger. My heart yearns for the intimate whispers and compassion of old, dear friends—friends to cluck and shake their heads with sorrowing disbelief when they hear of such great trials I must bear. Who can comfort like an understanding friend; one who stoutly declares you worthy of much finer blessings; who can carry from your door the cancer of a bitter heart, and drop it effortlessly in the dirt when she departs, there to be ground to dust and poison you no more.

Bethlehem - land of my springtime, friend of my youth! There was I a child with berries on my lips and dirt streaked between my toes. There was I a young woman, frothing with giggles, and sighing with lovely dreams. Naomi with laughter in her eyes, and tender words forever on her lips. In Bethlehem was I a bride, proud of such a fine man as my Elimelech. There were my sons conceived by moonlight, and hushed whispers of our love. And there my sons first saw the dawn, and I became a mother in Isreal.

Home! Home to Bethlehem! Warm again, with love, and friendship's sheltering arms. Home to Bethlehem where memories spread their sweetness over the bitterness of today, and bend the years like wheels, until yesterday touches tomorrows heels.

THE STRANGER

Ruth:

I am here a stranger cast upon a strange shore. Curious glances follow after my path, and I know not but perchance some slight word spoken may unknowingly offend, and incur untimely wrath.

Hold fast my hand, my mother. Do not forget me in your joy. No husband have I to cover me from bold looks and whispered words. Hold fast my hand, dear Father, for my life is given to Thee, and I must walk uncertain paths and climb unchartered hills. I have not strength within myself for terror fills my heart, and I would hide my face within thy cloak as a child behind its mother.

Dear Naomi, thy people shall now be my people, but what of thy friends? Will they also love me because they first loved thee? Or will I always meet with scorn when I look into their eyes, for Moab holds no honor in this land. Will I yet be numbered with the fold and counted an Israelite? How long will their memories hold me chained unto my past? Will I be old and still be Ruth the Moabite?

But it is Harvest and I will go and follow quietly in the fields. The grain cares not to whose hands it yields.

Jazelle 81

IN THE FIELDS

Ruth:

The reapers come early to the fields, before the sun has barely blushed the sky. I am sleepy still, and stumble along following the other women to the fields. Huddled in the soft shadows of the earth, I watch them walk arm in arm. I hear their small bursts of laughter and low whispers of their secrets.

But I am not alone for I carry always in my heart memories of happy times passed. At will, I summon up the dear faces of my mother and my father, the childish giggles of my sisters, and I clutch them fast to feast upon their savor.

The grain begins to fall as the reapers cut their wide valleys with the scythes. I marvel at how much they do not catch; baskets of grain lie carelessly behind them like jewels spilling over from too rich coffers for beggars like me to glean. I belong to the widows, and so may glean the barley left behind, and fill my basket if I can.

My hands are sore from yesterday, and the day before, of grasping the rough stalks of grain. Soon the tenderness has turned to sharpened knives of pain, and my back is laced by lashes of pain's cruel whip. I cannot decide whether it is easier to stay stooped over, following the reapers steps, or use my strength in bending then standing to ease the muscle's strain. Ere long it is no matter, for either way my strength fades with the growning heat of day.

Thirst! I thought I had known thirst, but till now we have been happy strangers. Now he walks beside me blowing dust upon my lips, stroking my throat with dry fingertips, filling my nostrils with noonday sun, and breathing smoke into my mouth. I stand, and arch my back against the stiff bristles of pain. Father, look down on me thy daughter, and bequeath me courage as my endowment.

Money is no treasure though it buys the present pleasure. Beauty is no blessing; it turns to jealousy in other womens' eyes, and besides it too soon slips away like a faithless friend. Even children's and husband's love may end, and leave you desolate, your treasure stolen by death's harvest. Grant me none of these except as excess. Yea, it is best, if I may just one blessing name; grant me Courage to meet each day. Then let fortune curse me as it may; with Courage shall I yet a measure of happiness claim.

MY DAUGHTER

Naomi:

Ruth is the sweet daughter that I longed for as a young wife. But Jehovah blessed me with two sons only, and though they were my pride, yet was I lonely sometimes for the soft gentleness of a daughter. Only after these many days do I begin to see that the Lord has many ways of blessing, and His priceless gift to me is Ruth.

Ruth, the Lord formed thee from angel wings to give thee grace. From pure holy waters springs the fountain of thy heart. Love lights upon thee as a cooing dove, and courage leaves its kiss upon thy brow.

When I have been weary your kindness soothed me and gave me new breath. When I have been sad, your love brought me cheer. When I have been faithless, your innocence reminded me of God's grace, and when I grow old I pray that you will be near, that I may find my dawn sky in thy face.

"Who is the Moabite woman?" friends have asked me. "Do you not find her strange?" they say. "What debt does she repay by walking so long a way with you, her husband's mother? He is long dead. She is free to wed another, and why would she leave her own mother?"

I cannot say. I cannot tell them how thirsty you were for rightousness. How eagerly you sipped the cool waters of God's holiness. I cannot tell them of the many days we sat together, knotting rugs, cooking, scrubbing, and you, my daughter, groped and questioned, and leaped far beyond me in your grasp of things eternal. I cannot tell them of the humility I feel at touching spirits with a soul so pure as thine. So I only tell them. "Love made her mine." And I can only pity that they have not such love of their own sons wives; daughters, friends to delight their lives.

A SINGLE WOMAN, ALONE

Ruth:

Mother Naomi, there was a man, and he was kind to me. It was your kinsman, Boaz, the other gleaners whispered. He found me by the wayside gleaning with the others. He called me out, and I was afraid. Perhaps he should say I might not have part with the others, widows of his own land. But he called me by name, and gave me food by his own hand, and bade me eat and drink with his reapers. See what quantity of good barley they let fall along my path. I could scarce contain it in my basket.

I was careful not to speak too boldly as unbecoming to a woman with no husband. And I did not invite the glances of the men. I looked not to the right neither to the left, but straight ahead I kept my glance, and ever cast down my eyes before the men. I would not have Naomi chastened because her daughter was immodest.

Still I felt some strange looks from the women, and wonder if they are afraid of me somehow. Mother Naomi, I do not want their husbands! I want my own! And he, alas is gone too long! If they could only know how I miss my own beloved, they would not be so jealous of their men. If only they could sit beside me in the cool evening when I see my husband's face in the tree leaves, and hear his love words in the wind. They might they touch their own sweethearts more softly, and be glad that, for now, they too are not alone.

I only want their graces and a friend's hand. I only want to belong again with people who like my voice and hear my song with pleasure and smile when they glimpse my face along the road. I only want to be Ruth - not a Moabite, not a heathen cousin turned Hebrew. Ruth - a quiet woman, not much used to laughter, with just enough memories of love to feed me when I'm lonely, and just enough hope that there will yet be happiness for me hereafter.

A KINDLY MAN'S DELIGHT

Naomi:

Ruth, my daughter, tonight shall be the threshing of the grain, and Boaz shall sleep before the door of the mill to guard his harvest. Tonight shall he sleep, and beside him on the floor, beneath his cloak a girl shall creep. Yea, Ruth, I know you are not bold, and never should perform so forward a deed. Yet there is need. Boaz looks on you with tender eyes, my daughter. Can you be so surprised? Only you have not seen him wait and watch for a glimpse of you. Do you not think it strange the provisions he makes for you, another man's widow?

Yet he would never shame you by asking for your love. And you can only dream so long and Mahlon think of. Ruth, do not cast insult on your first love by never loving more. Was marriage such a miserable chore that you would not enter it again?

Well then, when Boaz sleeps tonight you shall give a kindly man his heart's delight, and lay you down beside his feet. Do not fear, he will no doubt be righteous, and certainly will treat you honorably. Time out of time - fortune's cruel blunder will he correct, and you again shall be a wife in Israel.

DEAR BOAZ

Ruth:

Dear Boaz! my old man husband you call yourself, and chuckle so, and pull at your long beard. Dear Boaz! I chuckle too, remembering how once I feared you, for you were rich and strong and respected in the land.

Here, sweet husband, lay your hand beside mine. Yours is strong and large, and mine would nestle quietly in thine. I am not fearful any more, but come to you like a tame bird to rest upon your shoulder. And are you a little older? What of that? So am I. Older, yes, and happier than anyone by right should be. You redeemed me from sorrow and lonely child-less hours. You brought me flowers of tenderness, of joy. An old man, you? Why dear, dear man, you are just a boy, a mere boy learning life's sweetness new, struggling ever to better express your love. I've seen you skip and jiggle your feet a bit in a funny little dance when you thought no one could see, and I by chance was watching from behind the olive tree.

Boaz, God is good, and so, I think, are you. How fortunate I, a stranger, prepared for hardship and thinking only to live for others, should find a man who delights to serve me, and has made me in my maturity a mother. Obed bears your gentleness, and cultivates your goodness in his heart. Old man husband, what think you? Can it be that we should be a part of some grand design? Yes, Obed shall be a man of God, and after him his son, and his, and his, until at last will there be one like thee in goodness and mercy and love - a redeemer of all who sorrow and faint. On his umblemished soul shall we paint our griefs and joys. Greater than the desert sun shall be his light, and he shall spring from thee and me - Ruth a Moabite.

REFLECTIONS

OF

MARY

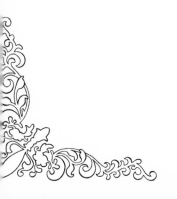

A ROYAL LINE

I was born of Ruth,
a royal line
from the time of David,
our greatest king.

I always mourned
that my father
did not call me Ruth, honoring
my ancestral grandmother.
For who is Mary?
But Ruth!
She is love and loyalty,
her name revered
by every Hebrew girl for humility.

But I am Mary,
and my father said,
"You must give honor
to your own name."
So all my life
have I endeavored
to be worthy of
so humble a name,
and so noble a lineage.

We are Nazarenes.
A tiny village, Nazareth,
and the people of Jerusalem
regard us not at all.
Yes, mighty deeds occur in Jerusalem,
but miracles in Nazareth!

Through the pale mist
of early morning's glow
I heard a song
begin and grow,
encircling me with silvery strains.
What was it?
Was it my name, Mary?
So it seemed,
and I almost thought I dreamed
the music was so compelling
and so dear.

But no, for as the music
fell enchanting on my ear
the song became an angel
and the angel spoke to me.

"Mary, it is time.
  The Son of God awaits
  at heaven's door his birth.
  A mortal temple shall you create
  for Him who first created earth."

But I was dumb,
  and only lately a child myself.
  "Can it be so,"
  I wondered, questioning, unafraid
  as children do.
  "With God all things may be,
  and He who formed the stars,
  and the earth, and sun
  shall transform thee
  into the Holy of Holies,
  wherein shall dwell
  God's own begotten son."

And I who never knew joy at all
  was filled with rapture
  until my very soul was quickened
  by glorious love divine.
  All the world fled away
  from beneath me,
  and I felt like a sparrow's feather,
  caught up and transported
  by a single, great warm breath —
  tumbling, spinning,
  drawn through space,
  half in life, half in death —
  until the world had passed away,
  all its sights and homely sounds,
  and only Heaven's starry blanket
  covered me.
  Exquisite light reached out,
  piercing through infinity,
  and touched my shivering soul
  with wild tranquility.

And I who never knew God at all
except in synagogues and evening prayer,
I met Him in eternity,
and knelt before Him there,
with all the planets and the stars
clustered at my feet.
And He accepted me,
and all the love I had to give
was pittance beside
that vast, consuming,
magnificent love of His.

ON THE ROAD TO BETHLEHEM

The road to Bethlehem is long,
And the way often rocky and steep
As it twists between the hills.
I am grateful for our placid donkey.
By day he bears me patiently,
And by night gives me
His warm side to lean upon
And try somehow to sleep.

Night falls upon us like a bandit,
Robbing us swiftly
Of the last moments of light.
Our little caravan settles down
Into the deep shadows of the night.
It would be a pleasant time —
Being with Joseph thus,
Under the stars,
Swimming in our dreams —
If it weren't for the surging
Wave of people, roaring
Through the canyons and valleys,
Tumbling over each other
In their homeward swell.

I am grateful to my Joseph
For loving me when others scorn,
For covering me
With the cloak of his honor,
And caring for me tenderly
As though I were the holy babe.
The others do not understand,
Even our own kinsmen whisper
About my untimely pregnancy.
How can they understand?
Even I am oftimes confused
And marvel at the power and the cause.
I know his friends
Often think Joseph a fool,
And he bears it all with dignity.

We cannot tell them
How it was many ages ago
When we three chose each other.
Jesus chose his brother, Joseph
As his earthly father, and Mary
to be his sister-mother.
Jesus, Joseph and Mary —
We bound ourselves with cords
Of love so strong
That we would share the joys
And the burdens willingly
From Bethlehem to Calvary.

No, even our kinsmen would not comprehend,
And the moment is too precious
To share with aught but deity.
So we travel somewhat apart,
And Joseph coddles me.
Father sends us gentle weather,
And I do not suffer much.
Only now, toward the end,
My back is weary,
And the child increasingly heavy within.
Did Mother Eve live thus
With just the clouds and winds
And animals for friends?
Oh, to sleep again in comfort,
Albeit a strange bed and strange room.
Ruth found kindness in Bethlehem;
Perhaps Mary may also soon.

IN THE STABLE

He who is the perfect love
    of all the ages
    permeates my being
    with His bright, exquisite love.
    O that I might hold him
    in my arms, and feast
    upon his beautiful face!
    And yet . . . yet to lose
    that fusion with Divine grace
    would be to desolate
    the soul of me.
    So I hold him jealously
    within my body.

My womb will not deliver him up
    to the careless world.
    When He is no more
    part of me
    he will belong to the universe,
    and I, who made his body,
    from my own
    will watch him grow,
    and go his way alone.

Joseph says there is no room
    for us in the inn.
    No room for Him
    who gave the earth its sun,
    and draws the majesty of heaven
    down to touch the earth!
    (Will my son
    be always so, an outcast
    in his own world?)
    Yet am I not surprised,
    for He who bringeth Peace
    should not be born in confusion.
    Indeed, all unholy noise should cease
    with this supreme fusion
    of Heaven and Man.

My heart is faint with fear,
O Father, can you trust your son
to one so young, so weak,
so inexperienced as I?
Might I not err
in my paltry efforts
of caring for the boy?
Yet it is true,
I have been prepared,
and all the sweet children
I have often rocked
have primed me for
this consumate joy.

I hear my mother's words
still ringing in my ears,
"Keep him warm,
and always by your side.
Breathe on him,
and the warmth of your love
will shield him
from harmful drafts
wherever you abide.
Be patient with yourself,
your body knows.
It will push him
from the security of the womb
into the security of your arms.
And soon the sweet milk will come
when sleepy head charms you
with his hungry tugs and whimpers."
O Mother, the time is here,
and now it is I;
I who whimpers,
and wishes you were near.

Father of my soul,
and Father of my child,
hast thou forsaken me
and left me all alone to weep?
For, behold, he cometh.
Glory goeth from my soul,
and my terrible grief is deep
as once my joy was wild.
For soon the Messiah will be born
in the darkness of the night,
and all my cherished light
given to the world.
O treat him tenderly,
this tiny babe,
this master soul,
seed of Deity.

BIRTH OF A CHILD

Silence descends.
A hush rolls out in waves
To the distant corners of the universe.
Somewhere across the breathless sea —
The everlasting eons of space —
Darkness suspends
The planets in somber graves.
But at God's throne brilliant spears of light disperse
To illuminate a galaxy
From the splendor of His face!

And stillness reigns.
A breathless quiet holds
The spheres and all expectant heaven waits
While God the Father brings to pass
The mystery of life create.
The power drains
From eternal fingertips, enfolds
The very particles of light of truth and penetrates
The birthing place of self-existent mass;
And Lo! A child of spirit generates.

Faint . . .
Misty . . .
Dim . . .
And dusky . . .
Drawing
Silver slips
Of light;
Fusing
Lustrous pearls
Of truth
'Til matter clings
To matter,
Emerging
Fluent
Unflawed
Primal Youth.

Gleam . . .
Glimmer . . .
Sparkle . . .
Shimmer . . .
Reflection of
Magnificent Sire,
Luminescent child of Celestial Fire!

Break forth! Resound!
Oh ye multitudinous worlds!
Ring out resounding strains of love divine,
For the Father holds another son,
Infused with glory, light sublime!
Roll forth! Rebound
Your cries of joy in rapturous swirls.
For Elohim his very Godhood doth refine
With each begotten spirit one,
Sons and daughters throughout all time.

And child
Of heavenly joy,
Hast thou come thus
To earth to be my boy!
Sweet one,
Sweet treasure mine,
Dost thou honor me
With a partnership divine!
Thy star
Has dawned on earth,
My morningstar,
First lighted at thy birth.

One child, one innocent soul
Of all the rest supreme.
He is my child; he is yours!
He is a grand creation's dream!

DISCOVERY

My child, greets his world, joyously,
like an old friend
whose dear charms have been unviewed
for too many long years,
and his baby face alights
at each friendship renewed.

In the small hours of the night
this wondrous child
who made his mother's world,
lies warmly curled
close by my protecting side.
Drops of sweet milk glisten
on his lips,
A soft, contented sigh
from both us slips.
And deep in ageless eyes I see,
that this matchless, mother's love
is a joyous discovery.

SACRIFICE

All Hebrew mothers
Consecrate their firstborn sons
To God's service,
And rest confident in their duty.
It is forty days,
And I take Jesus, my precious boy
In all his innocence and beauty,
And consecrate his life to man,
For he shall live for God
But, one day, die for man.

I do not always
See things so clearly.
Oftimes I wish I knew
Nothing at all.
But today the mists
Of ignorance flee,
And in the sacrifice of the doves,
I see my sweet son
As he will someday be,
The perfect, innocent, gentle offering;
The Dove of Heaven,
Sacrificed in ultimate charity.

THE MASTER BUILDER

Joseph is a carpenter,
A master craftsman in his trade.
He long has trained the young boys
Of the village to build.
He is not satisfied
Until they too are skilled,
And patiently he shows them how
You must plane and sand,
Selecting fine wood,
Shaping it into lovely, useful pieces
Bearing each the mark peculiar to your hand.

He waited for Jesus
To come of age to learn a trade.
Often hath he told me
"Mary, Jesus will be my best pupil.
He is young,
But he sees everything.
He knows all the tools
And how they should be used."

I am amused
To watch them from the doorway,
Joseph so tall,
Jesus still small,
But following after,
Learning even now
To be a Master Builder,
To shape the piece
And sand the flaws
And make a useful thing
From a block of wood.
Oh yes, he will be a Master Builder.
In truth he always hath been,
And inevitably will leave his mark
Upon the hearts of men.

THE QUENCHING

Today the wildflowers
Were a beauteous confusion
Leaping, gold and red, over stones
Up the hillside.
Jesus and I pulled each other
Up to the highest protrusion
Of rock, and languished
'Til eventide,
Basking in the glory of the view,
Fertile Gallilee upon the right hand,
And on the left,
A great sea of opalescent blue.

"Mother," he said, "See there,
The trees and flowering shrubs
Beside Lake Kinnereth.
See how they crowd the shore,
Struggling for a drink
Of water cool.
Someday a multitude
Of thirsting, struggling men
Will come in search
Of eternal cleansing water,
And I will be the quenching pool."

JOSEPH, A FATHER

Joseph was gone all day with Jesus,
Fishing in the waters of Galilee.
I worry when he is gone so far.
I fear the dangers of the road,
And of the sea.
So many caravans come and go
Along the roads of Galilee,
And a strong young man
Would bring a handsome price.
There are evil men abroad
Who if they knew his heritage
Would kill him in a thrice.

Tonight as he lay sleeping on his mat
I looked at him with heavy heart
That anxiousness had left.
Joseph came and stood by my side.
"Never have I seen so many fish,
They seemed to leap into his hand
And swarmed about us on the tide.
Mary, sometimes I choke with fear."
"I know," I cried, my courage all undone.
"O Mary, not for him,
Angels watch his every step.
For me, such an awful honor
To be the earthly father to God's son."

TRANSPORTED

Dawn tiptoes across the sky
On tender feet sunburned pink
From yesterday's sunset.
This morning Jesus came
To get me early
So we could watch the dawn together.
On the way up the hill
We found a bird's feather,
And from the summit he let it go.

Down, down it drifted,
Through the shadows,
Between the rocks,
'Til suddenly a wind arose,
Caught it up,
And lifted it above the earth,
Higher and higher,
'Til it was lost from view,
Transported on unseen power
Off into the blue.

"Do not fear the shadows,
Mother," he said.
"They may be fierce,
And I be dead,
But God can take me too,
And bear me up beyond the blue,
And like this feather,
Drawn into the skies,
Though I die,
Yet will I rise."

LEAVETAKING

The room is small, too small
for all the friends
and kinsmen who would bid
goodbye to Jesus.
Over the years
he often went with Joseph
on journeys to Jerusalem
to Acre, to Tiberias,
looking for good wood,
new tools, and new buyers.
and no one came to say goodbye then.

But now he has given the shop
over to his brothers,
and word has gone about
that Jesus will go out
and join John in the Jordan
baptising men to God.

So the town comes,
the old men and the little children,
the young men with their brides.
They stop and say,
"God go with you."
They do not know
they speak so truly.
They do not understand
why their hearts are so cast down,
but holiness goes out
when Jesus goes away,
and tomorrow Nazareth
will be a poorer town.

Finally the last one is gone;
the candle has burned low.
All night have I watched his face,
and he avoided my eyes.
Now he moves, slowly,
as though he were enwrapped
about by chain.
Now he comes to me
and kneels beside my chair,
and tears begin like tender rain.

"O son, I could be happy
    to see you go, knowing
    you were going
    to John and Jordan.
    But that is not so!"
He shook his head, wearily, "No,
    there is much beyond John."
"How much?" I asked.
"How long will be your ministry?"
But he only looked at me, silently,
    and kept his peace.
"Are all the good years passed?"
I asked.
"Will you ever have happiness again?"
"Not much," he said.
"But sometimes I will find a soul
    that will balance out the pain."

"O if only I could go with you,
    and share the hardships,
    and make a little nest
    where you might rest
    when you are sad and weary.
    I would share the sorrow
    that hangs about you like a sheet.
    I could lift it for a little
    and let you rest,
    and wash your feet
    when they are tired and slow."

He put his finger to my lips,
    and shook his head.
    "Mother, you cannot go.
    You cannot be a mother now,
    and I cannot be your son.
    When I leave your door tomorrow
    I shall belong to everyone.
    I shall be weary,
    and more in my heart than my feet.
    I shall be lonely,
    and shall with scorn and hatred meet.
    But, Mother, this is the purpose.
    This is the reason I came.
    Men will know my name
    and they will hate it,

or they will love it,
and both men must I reclaim,
both redeem from their mortality
that they may come to God
as I go to Calvary."
"Only promise me that you,
the dearest soul I know,
will not be foolish, and go
to see me at the end.
It would be too hard
to see you cry.
Perhaps my will would bend,
and I renounce the whole world
for your tears.

"No," I cried,
   "I cannot promise such a thing
and make myself a liar
when my son is dying.
If this is to be the crowning
of your divinity
I will be there with you,
not hiding like a coward.
After all, I too
belong to that moment
as I belonged to Bethlehem."

He put his head down in my lap,
   and wept as he never had before,
and I could only pat his hair
in my simple mother's way.
Whether he wept for me,
or for himself,
or for the world outside my door
I cannot say.
But this is when we parted,
truly parted;
and the next day
at early dawn when he started
down the village road
I did not cry,
nor did he,
for we had said goodbye
last night;
goodbye until Calvary.

ELDER BROTHER

Stories come home
That Jesus is making the blind to see,
That he is casting devils out,
And chasing moneychangers
From the holy temple.
They say that both the wise men
And the simple
Love him and follow after.
Of course, there are also those
Who hate him,
And shower him with cruel laughter,
Wishing him evil for his good.

His brothers and sisters ask
If I would not care to go and see.
But they are also dear to me,
And I will let my firstborn go
While I remain here with the family.
His brothers, too,
Are skilled at carpentry.
He and Joseph taught them well.
James and Simon sometimes wave to me,
And I can scarcely tell them at a distance
From their older brother.
Jesus gave to them his whistle,
And his delight
In lilies and birds in flight.
They cock their heads
As they have often seen him do,
And labor in the work shop
In his identical pose.

A brother or a sister knows
The purity of a brother's heart,
And they copy that
Which pleases them the most.
Last week I saw James,
Dear James, standing at a post
Reaching up to hammer in a nail.

A chilling wave rolled through me
And shook me as a boat without a sail.
And I sharply cried out,
"James, leave the thing alone.
Come son, I need you home!"

They have all begged him and me
To let them also go
And walk with him through Galilee.
But I am selfish
More than wise;
I could not bear to lose another.
For the Spirit whispers to me constantly
That which I fear most;
That we soon will lose our elder brother.

ON HIS MIRACLES

Miracles fall from His fingertips
Like translucent drops of love,
Raining sweetly on the earth.
Stars and angels at his birth,
Heavenly voices and a Holy dove,
Eternal water for thirsty lips.
Come sweet droplets, fill thou the cup,
And we like beggars drink it up.

ANGUISH

Open heaven's anguish,
Pour forth the rains
And cleanse the body of your Lord.
Pour thunder out across the sky,
Its roar is earth's reward
For the word of God is silenced now!
Then how shall God speak?
With lightnings and with thunder,
'Til the hinges of the earth shall creak
And crack the earth asunder.

O God, what part of the universe
Hides you; where have you fled?
Can you leave me with him all alone,
With our son, Jesus, dead?
He cried to you at the last
And did you leave him?
Could you leave him?
Did you flee and cast
Your heart beyond the rim
Of heaven into awful darkness?
I am blind, show me the way
And I will come and stay
Until a few eternities are past.

My firstborn son is dead!
I clutch his precious head
To my bosom and my heart tears.
Every mother bears
Within her soul
Her children's pain.
Then how shall I live
When my darling one is slain?
The same sorrow that killed him
Come now for me!
Or must I wander down the labyrinth of night
A beggar of death's charity?

O Jesus, Jesus, son
Is it all done,
All that began
Such long years back in Bethlehem?
Is it all gone
The joy you gave me
As my sweet baby back in Bethlehem?
Let me rock you once more, my angel,
There, there little boy,
Mother's near,
No terror of the night can touch you
With mother here.

Come down, ye black clouds!
Break upon my head.
Beat upon my stubborn soul
And make me, like him, dead.
For how shall I live with Jesus gone?
How shall anyone live
Without him,
Who came to earth
His perfect life to give?

Jesus, my son,
My Lord,
The gift is given
And thy mother's heart riven!

REFLECTIONS OF MARY

Long years ago
When I was yet a child,
I heard the Rabbi reading
From the prophet Jeremiah,
And I dreamed a singular dream —
That I would be the mother
Of the promised Messiah!

The years have brought much sorrow,
And too few smiles,
And the roads I walked with Jesus
Were poignant miles.
But far more aching now
Are the endless hours
I now endure apart
From Him and Joseph,
And my Heavenly Father.
For I was spoiled with divinity
And would rather
Live with them,
Whatever worlds they now roam,
Than wait behind this mortal veil
For my aging dust to fail
And my spirit to go home.

O did he die, this God-child,
This one Holy Man?
Was it a dream
From which we may recover?
No!
It was no dream.
For I am Mary, His mother!
And I was there at Bethlehem,
And gave my soul for Him.
I was there at Calvary
When He gave His soul for me.
And through all the years
That yet may be
I will testify unto the end —
All men come to earth
To live and die,
But Jesus,
He came not to live,
But to Live Again!!